How To Find All Missing Persons / Unsolved Cases. And Collect All Reward Offers. Volume XIV. THE CASE OF FELICIA MARIA WILSON

DAVID GOMADZA

www.twofuture.world

Copyright © 2024 David Gomadza

All rights reserved.

PAPERBACK ISBN: 9798326724915

DEDICATION

To a better futures

CONTENTS

How To Find All Missing Persons /
Unsolved Cases.
And Collect All Reward Offers. Volume XIV
THE CASE OF FELICIA MARIA WILSON   1

The Afterlife Conversation

and The Council Of Creation.   5

The Killers.   22

ACKNOWLEDGMENTS

Tomorrow's World Order

How To Find All Missing Persons / Unsolved Cases. And Collect All Reward Offers. Volume XIV. THE CASE OF FELICIA MARIA WILSON.

BACKGROUND INFORMATION

CASE

CATEGORY

$1m Reward, Cold Cases

DATE

10 Jan 1979
DESCRIPTION:

19 years of age.

Fair skin.

167 cm tall.

Slim build.

Long brown hair below her shoulders.

Wearing a beige coloured knee length skirt, a white blouse with a flower motif and a black and silver necklace. She was carrying a dark coloured handbag

How To Find All Missing Persons / Unsolved Cases. And Collect All Reward Offers.
Volume XIV. THE CASE OF FELICIA MARIA WILSON

1. 19 years of age.
2. Fair skin.
3. 167 cm tall.
4. Slim build.
5. Long brown hair below her shoulders.
6. Wearing a beige coloured knee length skirt, a white blouse with a flower motif and a black and silver necklace. She was carrying a dark coloured handbag.

QUICK CASE FACTS:

1. Felicia went to work at 8.25am on Wednesday 10 January 1979.
2. Felica was her usual self during the day and left work at 4.30pm to walk home.
3. Felicia did not return home at the expected time of 4.45pm.
4. Felicia's fiancé attended Felicia's address at 6.20pm but was told she had not returned from work.
5. Felicia's fiancé searched for Felicia but when she could not be located, he along with her parents report her missing to Police.
6. At about 8.00am on Thursday 11 January 1979 Felicia was located deceased by work colleagues in the bush area behind her work place in Kwinana.

CASE DETAILS:

Felicia Maria WILSON, was born in October 1959. She lived with her parents in Orelia and was due to get married in February 1979.

Felicia Maria WILSON was only 19 years old when she was murdered whilst walking home from her work on Wednesday 10

How To Find All Missing Persons / Unsolved Cases. And Collect All Reward Offers.
Volume XIV. THE CASE OF FELICIA MARIA WILSON

January 1979.

Felicia commenced work at the Kwinana Community Health Centre (KCHC) on Monday 8 January 1979.

At about 8.25am on Wednesday 10 January 1979 Felicia left her home address and was dropped at work at the KCHC by her father. During the course of the day she was in good spirits and carried out her duties as usual.

At about 4.30pm on this day Felicia left her work address and was last seen by her work colleague who stayed behind to lock up the premises. Felicia's work colleague saw Felicia walk past a window and onto a footpath in front of the KCHC. This is the last known sighting of Felicia alive.

On the day of her death, Felicia is believed to have walked along a bitumen pathway which leads through light bush land towards the Kwinana Shire Office building. It was approximately a 15-minute walk from her work place to her home address in Orelia.

Felicia's fiancé and her parents attended at the Kwinana Police Station at about 8.00pm that evening where they submitted a Missing Person's Report.

Felicia's family and the police conducted searches of the area in an attempt to locate Felica.

The following morning, Felicia's work colleagues conducted a search of the bush behind KCHC and located Felica deceased in a small clearing of native bush approximately 70 metres from the bitumen path.

The person or persons responsible for Felicia's death have not yet been identified despite a very long and intensive investigation.

https://www.crimestopperswa.com.au/open-cases/homicide-felicia-maria-wilson-kwinana/

TOMORROW'S WORLD ORDER'S PERSPECTIVES THE AFTERLIFE CONVERSATION AND THE COUNCIL OF CREATION'S ANAYLSIS.

I had just finished work when my fiancé phoned and said he won't be coming home soon was at work as well so i said okay he left and went i don't know where before i arrived when i arrived he was there but sad saying he lost the job but he can get another soon i quickly walked back to work that same afternoon to speak yo my supervisor about work for him or extra work in overtime now as i approached the work he followed and said don't ask them because it will embarrass me if they are to know that i lost the job i can find a new job without them knowing okay so i agreed and were returning home when he said let's fuck and i said when we get home we can fuck so he held my hand and begged and i said yes so we went in the bushes and had 4 times sex doggy style first and then 3 missionaries and i dressed up before i know it he hit me hard in the head and said die i can get life insurance money and i just died there and there without a word or a bye it hurts really hurts now if i ask everyone why my own fiancé would kill me they say it's insurance money but what insurance money because i don't have any insurance money i worked for a clothing company called stermmnopqrst or daisy clothes there was no mention as insurance at all if i knew i would have cancelled it someone warned me to be careful of him and he said i can get the money and send you in hell while you wait for the judgement and i said how long is that he said for 120 years and i sat down in my hell holding area and said where is all this about money why i need here in hell there is so much darkness you hardly see anything and all i here are voices of crying people saying it's really hot please reduce the hell fires the meat evaporated what's left is just my soul and it hurts i faint 1000 times per day please tell my beloved ones never to come to hell i beg them to do right things now i ask what is this insurance money and why i am still in hell people who are coming say it's 2024 so what's going on since 1979 this is not right help me at least let me know what is going on and how long i am going to be here okay that's my case i died on 11 january 1979

there was no long ago start soul died inside you it was trapped

How To Find All Missing Persons / Unsolved Cases. And Collect All Reward Offers.
Volume XIV. THE CASE OF FELICIA MARIA WILSON

the blow to the head wa6s so severe that i died without doing anything checking now i just realized that i died first before her something that should not happen and it say this is the first time in the history of creation when this happened never had a soul died first this is the first time this happened no long ago calculated or anything u remember a voice message saying if i can you can but who donit is the password to the riches but first take care of the body as i said now if we can how can they one must fail either us or someone else never mind god i diverted all the messages to send.ya and if you do it right you will not need to worry about anything because all you need is to hit the head at right angle to it so stand on her side and wait for her to bend down at least at 33 degrees and then hit her hard while at that angle the brain won't register anything but at anything else then you will have lost because you are going to spend all this time in jail now let's look at what we said before take her back to work after reaching home then she never come back two strip all clothes and put new clothes in her jacket pocket when you cum don't come inside her wear plastic and don't ask anything any unresolved issues the brain will remember when she wakes up she will feel like she never died forever and does god have places for semi alive people who can function like humans without bodies if not then what can be done you said i wakeup and zit in my holding area i literally sit down and stand and walk around in my grave holding area describe it its like a single room you sit shit urinate and ask questions people who work there who are in white robes who only say Yahweh the other side is for people who wear dark clothes and they say only auuuuuha and disappear now what i asked is this can someone tell mr why its been so long and why it hurts just to sleep i went to the other side not knowing what us what and saw all of them sleeping but not moving at all when i said who killed you they all refused to talk about their deaths i can't remember how i died so the question is what is to be of me and when waiting is the most killing and hurtful then if i can go somewhere where can i go and when
why you kill your own fiancé i was broke then there was a possibility of making it big she said she would do anything for love this was the

How To Find All Missing Persons / Unsolved Cases. And Collect All Reward Offers.
Volume XIV. THE CASE OF FELICIA MARIA WILSON

love i had in mind the better her death refused she had any insurance and so she died for nothing anyone who put you up to this to challenge god etc? Why challenge god no need what was said was that can a human being die but still think it's alive enough to wait for things people who are alive wait for my heart say yes if he think money is more important than my life then let him get the money but from where unless he meant that cltert life insurance i once had but i cancelled that one because someone at work frightened me he said cancel life insurance before at killed atmos was his name short for atmospheric pressure first name and second name he choose this name himself what was his re name abey tlort born on 28 of dumber 1963 as he put it but wanted something smooth
identified as felicia wilson maria and fiancé abey torture of denver australia electromagnetic wave number for abey tlort is 8928386872867892801389028678100386782198773857890132748921 0832846890183
his phone number 778638678280198365489018274183 his house is 2798386 hunting denver australia age range 68 to 84 the house in felicia maria wilson value 278980183289 bought in 1978 in november on a loan of 278980386 but when she died did not change ownership abey had to change name to atmospheric pressure to cover for the pressure he put in getting the house but not in his name trying to trap her into later giving up the house the company she worked for daisy clothing keeps monthly repayments until now secretly so abey won't lose the house because he kept saying that she will come back as someone else on rebirth to take back the house do you want to come back to earth i came and didn't like it you finance kept hoping that you would come back one day is it possible? Can you look in your fiancé's eyes i am in after life i can't okay this is another case that challenged how the court handled cases like this we looked at all possible outcomes to find out how we can look at this case now one thing is certain a young beautiful life has been stolen in broad daylight by her own finances someone to trust but in this case the enemy so harsh that she didn't die as our records show when death came she was in another world

when it left it was something rose to her now the was she speaks its like you are talking to someone alive does Yahweh have a special place for people like her? If we look at this case its one of the most heartbreaking cases of all time because the woman even in death she still loves the fiancé that she us still willing to sacrifice her time waiting for him to get the money to pay for the house so that they will be together so she said it's hard waiting i wake up and walk and sit but i tell you the waiting is the hardest part she is dead but her brain did not die so she asks questions as if alive this is the first time we have seen something like this now what can be of her this is the answer forever she will be traumatized by the waiting in such a way that she sees all this as the hardest thing to do now what can be of her after this she could remain there or go to heaven now what can be said about her if this had not happened she could be happily married now but probably

court of creation

this case has brought challenges 11 jan 1979 at 22.20am Yatime to the court and is designed by humans to test Yahweh and his superiority and ask several questions regarding how the court is run is the court run on just facts and as a matter of fact or subjective where evidence from one case can be substituted for another here we see a case where faith is tested to extremes and where principles are challenged we believe in dealing with a case on its own merit and where there is little evidence then we can always ask others what can be said about this case is the fact that it has all the hallmarks of a fake case enacted to waste the court's time but as it will turn out it is to challenge use of predefined systems alone as a way to judge humans what if the predefined system did not work then what so we are going to look at what predefined systems that did not work and how to rectify this situation and the way forward it is like humans are rewriting the creation manuals again and test the creator to find out how he would react and what other ways to use where a predefined parameter fails now what did fail

1. The send.ya message system failed no chance at all for a message the time was too short for anything

2 the alarms system did not work at all

How To Find All Missing Persons / Unsolved Cases. And Collect All Reward Offers.
Volume XIV. THE CASE OF FELICIA MARIA WILSON

3 the bird crying system did not work at all
4 the brain sending message did not work at all
5 the soul escape system did not work at all
6 the brain recording function did not work at all
7 the human voice analysis system in the soul and the geographical positioning system did not work at all
8 the voice recognition pattern system in the brain did not work at all
9 the alarms of death that include the famous long ago start did not activate at all
10 the human signaling system did not activate at all
now what can cause 10 warning systems all to fail at the same time as we looked at this case it raises number of questions was this a deliberate attack with intention to challenge the creator or an accidental misshapen something we ruled out outright for this to be an accidental mishap something must have happened first to lock everything i mean all 10 clever predefined settings created by the almighty majestic Yahweh now humans recently have tested Yahweh and said we can do better than him at one point one tried to grab him and send him to hell now what can be of humans that fight the creator evil and without a good solid foundation and leadership for they are lost because no matter what humans forever will be mortal without Yahweh only Yahweh can give them extra years on earth now what does this case say about humans humans over the years have become frustrated by the help system as part of the predefined system because that help function had not been answered even once by Yahweh since creation and his reasons are that imagine if he has to answer every call of help with thousands dying on a daily basis that would stretch the resources after all a person is guided by how they live disobey the predefined characters and end up dead hence no point complaining because those who follow the predefined parameters live up to 100 years so if he is to blame then what about these are they special or just lucky 80 % of the population who follow predefined parameters live up to 100 years so the predefined system in that area works now let's look at each above parameter and find out why it has failed and whether

How To Find All Missing Persons / Unsolved Cases. And Collect All Reward Offers. Volume XIV. THE CASE OF FELICIA MARIA WILSON

deliberate or not the first one failed because the send.ya message was diverted to another port namely pc arterp anterntop who left a message saying that i quote Yahweh can't be reached now but you can contact pc arterp aternop who can answer pronto now let's look at this message in detail the diversion is meant to prove that Yahweh is as good as away as can be therefore calling for help from him will only be a waste of time and will cost you your life because there is no way he can come to the rescue if he can let his son jesus be killed by humans that means his systems will not work for you now this is common among humans to attribute a prophet as god's son because they killed him and showed him power jesus as far as we all can remember was one of the great prophets of his time but he never was Yahweh's son but his messenger even though then they were close in communication god declared that he doesn't want human children he has his beautiful catitighit whom he loves greatly but the idea of humans as children of gods is sickening and inappropriate humans die so where are the godly genes if one was a god the father in this case where is the intelligence that the gods posses genes don't vanish just because you mated a lower grade but might actually upgrade that where is the i never die attitude of god's in jesus this all is insulting to the gods hence to prove that jesus was not a god but just another abandoned human to be saved during the Pharisees time was associated with godliness so that the phrases won't think of killing him and when they did find out that there was nothing godly about him they challenged everyone and said if he is the son of a god then they thought Zeus then let Zeus appear as we nail his son on the cross this was a direct challenge to the gods as it was look if the ground is lower that you can't see then look down we can even lift him up and nail him so fast with the hugest nails so that his cries for help would rich you secondly we will leave him there firv3 days the significant number of gods to appear before Yahweh's court of creation now what happened after three days they had to send humans to steal the corpse to avoid further humiliation that jesus was indeed just another human being look at his taste of women there is nothing godly about that he picks the worst of all for companion excuse me a god with wealth

How To Find All Missing Persons / Unsolved Cases. And Collect All Reward Offers.
Volume XIV. THE CASE OF FELICIA MARIA WILSON

would not do that but would go for the best now if we ask what happened after he was laid to rest that is decayed and be buried this is not typical of gods look at the next thing to gods in Ibrahim he was lighted to heaven and never decayed once you decay then where is the godliness in this humans have failed to think it's like in creation where they say man evolved from apes but those apes are still there if there was evolution then the apes would have extinct and all become humans now let's look at why the send.ya message failed a simple code was used to divert and the code is in digits as the brain makes commands easy it converts long functional parameters into number codes and then give the codes a simple name so that instead of reciting all the numbers in this case it simply says divert01 this is the code 08987654832109842678268489018278678099887762892 now let's ask what can be done with this another code can easily be applied to remove this if we simply say undo send.ya message diverts the brain will create another code that removes and call it divert02 meaning is opposite of the one before this and the code is 03698765890028698320184869286700 now what this does is to remove the first code and add this as the new code now the messages can now go to the creator Yahweh then this would mean that now the creator can receive the messages in this case the pc aretop said that he can let all dying people not to even bother about sending the message but by trying to save themselves in that situation all the seconds one spend calling Yahweh must be used to escape instead in this case he was right something the court acknowledged and said she spent 4 seconds making the call with no answer instead if she had run out first then call then she would have sent her soul instead to Yahweh and ask the time bit takes for the souk to get an answer is long making the system ineffective and the court asked if there was anyone answer to this system Yahweh did not answer instead said i will fix it if it's that bad now if we look at why souks are becoming scarce and scarce is that people have put too much trust in Yahweh when Yahweh is never there to act now if there is another way to deal with this issue when humans die a lot of things you take for granted dies as well with death but what if we

How To Find All Missing Persons / Unsolved Cases. And Collect All Reward Offers.
Volume XIV. THE CASE OF FELICIA MARIA WILSON

can clone all humans now when all are alive then create an afterlife where these clones live happily ever after and when original is in trouble that sets alarms to the clone to act and go back first to the owner entry opens all ports just as the alarm systems we tested this and that let's the original souk out and they can emerge again into one and this goes to Yahweh this is feasible in our time now let's look at the second issue now if we look at what happened at first its beyond comprehension how a soul would [cloning up to 3 maximizes strength] die first Yahweh's predefined parameters this is not to happen at all and to Yahweh's credit this has never happened before for all years since creation and that is a very long time now let's look at why the soul died first the soul said i can't breathe someone ask Yahweh why this is happening is this in the predefined system because i failed to locate that part in the manuals maybe let me check again and it said check.start.canvibrationsbecontrolledbeforedeath.start instantly there was an answer yes say i did not wear vibrations only the human did and proceed but when it said i did not wear the human it actually died because this removed the human environment and it died this is part of the predefined now what this did was to9 remove the human conditions that keeps it alive what does a soul need air water and o0 to fly does it have wings yes but in electromagnetic form now what can be of the course here is that it needs electromagnetic waves to keep alive now if removed that trigger cardiac arrest in the soul that means death can you give cpu to electromagnetic waves [you can use this code to create electromagnetic wave conditions 82698789018324867890183678928401836890182489018683861900 or divert84] now what can be said about all this is the fact that if we are to ask what can be of souls without electromagnetic waves the answer is death now we are just looking at several conditions first as required by the creation council manuals namely 08986789012348628901846587901842862789018678918 3210 now what this say is that to keep the souk alive humans must generate enough electromagnetic waves to channel to the brain to keep the soul alive now what can cause this shortfall its a sudden

How To Find All Missing Persons / Unsolved Cases. And Collect All Reward Offers. Volume XIV. THE CASE OF FELICIA MARIA WILSON

disruption of all brain function this we noticed that can happen only at an angel called the trajectory of death design by default meaning this was god's plan from the word go to find a solution where if faced with stubborn humans he can easily use this tactic to immobilize them and stop them from thinking and control them now what happened is that on this day abey the fiancé practiced angles at home with her saying help me if i don't i might be sacked all of a sudden at work now they insist on these things which i have now forgotten now what are these angles he tried angle 30 degrees so hard on her that she started asking why 30 with no effect or response all he had to do now was to add a 3 degrees to make sure that it becomes the trigger of death instead of anything therefore preserving the brain and everything else so thereby killing only the body and living the brain literally alive now what can be said of her after this she will be so alive that her actions would resemble that of all humans alive but her body dead now what is the effect of that on her this is to keep her alive to remember everything than death itself so she can't tell whether she is alive or dead but in that state there are things she can say she can do but these are only brain emotions she can say i sat down this is because that function is there but without a body how is that possible so we ask why the need for her brain alive we looked at things like secret codes passwords etc now what can be said about her now even though she is dead she can think and remember just like any living human being only that she does not have a body now what can be of brains without bodies a new science has emerged where computers etc uses a human dna to power a scheme like i proposed the same with our twitter version where my 53 billion 800 dna that that resembles god's to be used as hard drive for the twitter roots and trees which can be success considering i have managed to put this dna on a disk and on youtube as an mp3 that's so cheaper than proposed quantum computers now the effect is to use her as a filing system in death one can simple ask her questions and retrieve information they need from her like secrets etc so the first suspect obviously would be the company she worked for who taught her everything on discovering that the fiancé has lost the job now fear that she

How To Find All Missing Persons / Unsolved Cases. And Collect All Reward Offers. Volume XIV. THE CASE OF FELICIA MARIA WILSON

would relocate if he finds a job somewhere else and run away with their secrets now what kind of job did she do this is the answer she was in the clothing business making cutting and sewing clothes for women and hard started the company herself only to be bought out when the fiancé proposed but having been paid handsomely enough to afford a house that means she was a house owner and had secretly paid it in full at 2789083201 in 1979 just before she died but had kept it a secret after someone warned her that her fiancé was once engaged to someone with a house and they split up and she died before they changed the house name as he had put the name in his name after she had paid some of the money then refused the house as noisy neighbors and hot the money and changed name to atmospheric pressure to cover the rumors of him pressuring his fiancé to pay for the house but put it in his name her ending up disappearing now she rung a one atms and said i finished work where are you can you pick me up and he said okay but i am already home if you can come fast home i have bad news to tell you this was to make her cut all her routine of visit friends on the way home now after she arrived he said i lost the job but i can find another fast i just thought i tell you so that you don't spend money unless you have to that made her suspect that the cat was out of the bag now if we ask what can be of her at this point then this is the answer she could be as dead as a stone because once he finds out that they had bought her out that means she is rich and now her life would be at risk now what can be of souls without great stamina she said her soul was training for extra time inside in case she gets stuck inside who trains her soul that was unless there is a risk of
think
dying that way i think she researched how she died or disappeared and acted upon that information that she trained up to fight till death i think this is what as a counter triggered the need to cause vibrations so that the training would be useless now how can you counter a souk that can stay in the body for as long as she can a huge wave of vibrations that kill soul firs and fast so that it can't send messages to Yahweh so that no one knows exactly what happened now if we ask what can be of souls that die first now this is the answer souks that die first will forever be dead because they have not triggered life

How To Find All Missing Persons / Unsolved Cases. And Collect All Reward Offers.
Volume XIV. THE CASE OF FELICIA MARIA WILSON

after death a souk exists because it triggers life after death switch in order to start that life it must say create.start.lifeafterdeath.start if this is not done then there is no life after death as death will only be the system in its predefined system like what god said this is the only case in the entire history of creation and you will find out why soon now if we ask what can be of souks that don't register the start of a new life when they die everything dies with them threatens that if we ask a souk to start after death without this brain start then it will never start unless if you are Yahweh himself or his representative who can resurrect it from death meaning restarting everything by this command
restart.asbefore.start.now.newlifeusingknownconfigurations.start when this start then new life will have been added and the more you repeat the greater the new life and this is the secret to longevity for humans alone everything else is a fuss
you must ask the right questions you must do the tasks what tasks
1 be the creators representative
2 ask him for long life like him
3 ask why humans die
4 say i can do the same as you here on earth
5 say i can and will as per your commands Yahweh
6 ask for human sin forgiveness
7 ask to end up with Yahweh in eternity
8 ask to represent him all over the universe
9 say i will and i shall
10 ask if we can add your name in the book of creation
now let's look what can be of Yahweh with people who test him according to him this is the first time humans have tampered with predefined systems to such an extend so as to cause death without ant trace now let's look at who and why would want to do this this is done for secrecy reasons let's say that if i want to use your dna secretly which is illegal but keep your brain and filing system working this is how we will do it kill and keep brain alive and continue that means since she is the owner of the company she literally embedded this dna in herself as a system so initially she volunteered as a new way to add all company clothes designs inside her and link everything to her when she sold the company they paid her handsomely even according to her brain scans this means that to

her it was handsomely but to them they bought living human dna which illegal to avoid murders like these so why this time she accepted to die so that fiancé can continue living in the house but if you are that clever and rich why not ask him to die and you live? If we go deeper we start to see a pattern here something was wrong with her she was sick this is the only thing that makes sense if she is sick she is going to die anywhere so she can accept this otherwise its a waste so instead of waiting for disease to kill her and destroy her she admitted to dying and preserving her brain to be used as a dna filing system that will live forever hence the huge payout now who would pay that handsomely and why the answer is an international company who had that she had veneered and instead hired her doctor to induce code 89876548386789018387788990123867890286 in her so that it kills everything first other than the brain meaning preserving dna and this is what happened even though she was not ill at all she admitted when her vagina fell in the toilet on 10 january 1979 the doctor had warned her that her things could literally fall while she is still alive she picked up her vagina and said holy mary mother of jesus what vagina done it was me you want not the vagina you bastard abey talking with doctor atkin to mess my genius plan for what i was going to marry you so that we share now i rot alive i swear if i can then and he walked in with her holding her vagina he said what's that smell i it's time to do you now can we please by tomorrow you will be in heaven what is good of your ideas all i need is a vagina so let's go put that in your pocket and let's go now before everyone finds out what happened its better to hear that someone killed you that that you killed yourself by your ignorance only you in the world why now if we look at what happened then this is not true this is the fiancé version now let's look deeper as to what that code does it eats away everything and leave threads of flesh hanging now what happened this day she was in pain and said can we fuck once to keep vagina alive longer and he said how longer the smell is now awful people have sex because there is attraction remove that and death follows i mean divorce and she cried and said he loved her because of her secret plan so he must not complain it comes with the package and she cried and fell asleep but a message woke her up it said i tried to work things out but we must end this madness ourselves if we let others get involved we will loose everything

How To Find All Missing Persons / Unsolved Cases. And Collect All Reward Offers.
Volume XIV. THE CASE OF FELICIA MARIA WILSON

meaning everything i loved you for as well the vagina the most and today it gave up imagine seeing it in your own hands this is traumatizing enough and i can kill myself and go to hell foe peace what did i do to deserve this my friend has nothing and he is happy he has a wife with a vagina and no house he never thought of killing himself at all i did this is the 78th time so tell me me or you it's okay i still love you i could have left the house is in your name i never change it so decide we can't go own again today the doctor your vicious evil doctor atkin phoned and said you will drop all genitals too because if you deep your dick after the vagina has fallen they will now stick onto your penis and i am scared i don't want anything from you just ... Brain check revealed a just kill yourself and rest you must forget about how your body was in the end i asked god and he only said 33 is the trajectory of death now if we ask is this the true no this is what he would have said if he knew what i know so what really happened that day he said doctor i am about to live to pick up my wife at work what should i say [bitch having sex with the devil behind my back and losing the vagina because the devil uses knives to fuck today i witnessed hell on earth i can never stop thinking about this] now the phone was on hold when a code arrived send.to.[abey.tlort].code878678901987645823816789018928648 and say ask what's for dinner and if she say meat pretend to throw up if she say vegetables salad say oh no how long can this shit go and move around like this and take the bins out now let's ask what can be in this case she could now admit that death is obvious and end her life but choose to forget about the deadly situation now what can be said about the situation we can assume that at this point after the vagina dropped down the only left thing is to go in peace before things get worse now what can be of her now that the worst has happened from this day after losing the vagina and promising herself not to tell him and only to walk in when she is about to eat it is not just horrible but an act of a clever manipulating magician watching as the drama unfolds now what can be of humans without genitals the worst feeling that leads to murder now let's look at what can be said about this situation at this point its a point of no return what could be can be now she could see death as the only option now let's see what can be of her and others around her if it is that bad then there is no more life death will be the only solution if we ask what

How To Find All Missing Persons / Unsolved Cases. And Collect All Reward Offers.
Volume XIV. THE CASE OF FELICIA MARIA WILSON

can be out of all this now if we ask her what are your thoughts at this point in time she says great but let really down my fiancé was to make me happy i had promised that if he had shown me real love i would kill myself and go to hell to sleep and wait for him in afterlife now ask what can be of her at this point in time she would be walking dead literally but what can be of her on this day she could be in hell buy noon now what can be of others they could not behave the same if we ask what was and what can be of humans without sex organs lost and pitiful to earn hell by default now let's conclude and reveal the real truth she was murdered fir her house by a doctor atkin who received a quarter of that money as donation from daisy clothing limited on 18 september 1978 the day she sold the company for 2896789 dollars but valued at 4 times that amount as having the world's first best filing system which was never released only until on 28 of december when her fiancé said holy shit you will die instead of kissing her and lifting her up if he had done this he was the one to die of whatever was to come to the system the commands to self preserve were ask for marriage but to someone who loves you for money and not love now say i won the lottery i hide the ticket inside me but lift me and shake me and become backup now if we ask what could have been after this this is the answer now if we ask what can be of humans with no regard of life for money this doctor atkin broke all safety regulations and killed a woman but one can argue that this is prosperous that he had anything to do with what behalf her but let's look deeper at this doctor he said if i can then you can to abey when he refused first time and said who do i fuck all that time you experiment your cancer drugs on her she has no cancer full stop and he said if you don't act now you will regret it she has no cancer so medicine will strengthen her say what if the system inside your dna turns cancerous who to blame and she will accept and lie and say the police might arrest me instead can you tell them that it was your idea and not mine all this to make her agree but she refused saying then who pay for those tests and in what name and he said i can change my name to atmospheric pressure for two months that means quitting my job and try you know i will do everything for you and he said okay only if that saves your life what they did not know was that the system had a secret recording that sends messages to the doctor even though it was not him who installed the system he had illegal hacked

How To Find All Missing Persons / Unsolved Cases. And Collect All Reward Offers.
Volume XIV. THE CASE OF FELICIA MARIA WILSON

despite being banned because he tried to hack into her to deposit vitals but was identified by a harsh tag which he refused to prove it was him the court ordered a simple reverse sending that meant sending back his vitals back to him which resulted in him getting the exact cancer he had predicted in her now let's look at all these messages to convince the court that all were his he said someone from daisy clothing sent me a cancer causing virus and it attacked me so fast i nearly died so the company send him a donation of 2867890 then he took it to court but in court the company now had to reveal everything and said she was attacked first but her defense system always sends back to sender as binaryreverse now let's see what can be of this situation the doctor got a test of his medicine and nearly died in two months that is 64 days but as a cancer doctor he saved his life but his genitals had fallen down and to make things worse he had lied that he was testing a drug when in actual fact he was trying to kill her so that when the company discovered this they paid him handsomely now so that he send the same code to her twice to disable the system so opening her for further him because she had put the system herself she had nothing to worry about but when they bought the company they removed her own system fir theirs and that window period he took advantage as the cheque reads we have changed owners we are now the daisy clothing company and full changes rake place in two days in the mean time systems might not be at 100 percent to a quarter so act fast if you still need some of the old systems but he refused until another undisclosed cheque arrived as a blank cheque saying for your janitors if you lost them that infuriated him and said i can for 9 digit figure in advance like 289678690 and they all looked lost in the conference meeting to address his queries but the manager understood and said we can quarter you if you can of that that means in layman's term if he can reduce the life of felicia maria wilson by a quarter they would pay him a quarter of that meaning a quarter of 289678690 which is 9868702 which is money never received because what the company did is now install her system just before she finds out but she had received a message as her predefined system that said you have received a mallard disguised code that can affect not this system but the new system permanently resulting in malfunction or system collapse and she squinted her eyes and said can i tamper with their

How To Find All Missing Persons / Unsolved Cases. And Collect All Reward Offers.
Volume XIV. THE CASE OF FELICIA MARIA WILSON

security as well and for the first time her own aty said it's your system that's started to be destroyed not theirs and realised what had happened but first checked system.searchformalwareandfix.start now if we check what happened this is what happened she said new daisy owners please fix mallard detected during transfer therefore your sole responsibility and the said okay we can switch off and reboot but you must wait for a restart okay then he said what can be done his aty said disconnect before contamination spread i think deadly cancer of the vagina detected and he laughed and said i am a man but suddenly stopped and called her and said is your vagina okay and she said touching it hard for pain and said so strong even avstud like you can't break it and he had a diadiafiadiadiadiadiadiadiadiadiadiadia that he said not joking i can come to yours in 10 and do you 2.5 and lose this thing how can i walk and she took off her knickers and massaged vagina standing with her knickers still on her ankles and said raw and ready long time a man has given me attention for my vagina all its for money this sucks i am pretty and instantly after 10 minutes a message was received and it reads 10 is perfect do make it 2.5 minutes to close the deal so what was happening was that the doctor received a copy through port using xtyrxyz then now what happened is that she noticed that the message was not meant for her because at 2.5 nothing happened as she had drooled so fast and hard mild squanks had started and she cursed talking to herself and said what the fuck who keeps a woman waiting like this the minute her fiancé entered the door and said what that smell who make you this horny how much does he have if you have 8 billion then he must have 2.5 more because 2.5 is all it is to squanks and squanks size and rounds she looked lost and grabbed him and for the first time had rough sex with him he was 8 years younger than her meaning only 11 years old but she said if you tell i kill you and hide you in my vagina and he said people have to cut it open then they all laughed now what can be said of women who abuse kids then no one support them and she said i want him for me but and he said okay my mother died of cancer my house repossessed and yours might be taken too and she said i adopted you you are my son and he said my mother died what if we get engaged then what and she refused and said who dies of cancer unless and he said it's a lie my mother never she was as good as you like a real son she adopted me for the house and she

How To Find All Missing Persons / Unsolved Cases. And Collect All Reward Offers.
Volume XIV. THE CASE OF FELICIA MARIA WILSON

said i don't know you have a house and he said what did you adopt me for i wonder you have the most expensive house in the country you were on news last week when you bought it after selling the house she said i was happy i wish i had a real son all along she was talking to her aty which she had named her finance abey tlort her password to her system and who later changed to atmospheric pressure now if we look at this case there are no kids involved the police to be believed in court as you nearly believed above use aty to provide drill- fills they will use in court but without her knowing to aim for prison sentences and justify the use of cancers by doctors involved and cover their acts there was no boy involved but aty a talking chatgpt using acetate us used to be a stand or placeholder for a real boy because on this day they hired a real boy to help her and take her for the walk now as the final days to be seen by this person and take secret pictures which they will give as evidence in court now the picture taken was presented to the boy and said her vagina fell in the kitchen and i ran out i had just return from school i cried so hard and at the same time on national television how did i do they all laughed and people started pointing fingers and said are they trying to steal her big house from you because if you are the adopted son they it should be in your name the doctor said i am her doctor to act as guardian sign here and he put an x and he was handed the keys up to now he is still waiting for her too whence he is no one knows but the house was taken as a crime scene were even though her body was found in the woods to protect the house from the thieving police they brought her body and said she wonder after being killed by her fiance now ask her to look into the eyes of her finance i never heard a finance it was a aty some talking thing that can shake you and imitate you but in mirror image now we can conclude and say that she died of a severe form of cancer that attacks genitals losing her vagina from. perfect to death in 64 days the most recorded recorded aggressive form of cancer administered as it turned out later by atm as preloaded at birth but why the reason an only child of a mother who owned the house and a father who owned a daisy clothing company therefore assassinated at radiation point all for the big house value on purchase by mother a one estilt vetursty meaning vultst now if we ask why the police according to their secret thoughts are entitled by an article called the protection of proceeds of capital

How To Find All Missing Persons / Unsolved Cases. And Collect All Reward Offers.
Volume XIV. THE CASE OF FELICIA MARIA WILSON

gains tax article 235 that's says any land owned by orphans must be repossessed at any cost and be kept to be given back at 18 years so the question is this was aty created to protect or to make it easy to steal from orphans or to kill and get away with murder ladies and gentlemen you decide but the facts speaks for themselves ask why these bad things happen to people with property?
The end

THE KILLER, THE CONFESSIONS AND THE COORDINATES

Felicia Maria Wilson detected electromagnetic wave number is 8398765836789018367800182386189100386286109384 now her address was 27893 terterst street Denver Australia she had a fiancé abey tlort current location 887766889983678098386780983827841980186387992862701842 890018 South of Denver Australia near uteretch ertcheterthet Australia in the sand saying I okay but where hmmm no answer now if we anaylse further its a computer chip stertertstuvw meaning xtpstp38678901836 her coordinates are 89689977886832108928378109286386170199876380286119 near much near her fiancé the chip board in metres 3.867890123486 metres away from her as she is in a cemetery called forever we will until God said otherwise in attack on God in local language stuvwxyzstuvwertstuvwstry meaning uteretcht Denver Australia
The daisy company helped the doctor cover for aty by acting through drills making it look like he was the one involved in administering the lethal drug covering for aty and the police especially Pc astern ajern in this case played by Pc tamnop who said at the time what could be of orphans with a small brain and a big vagina that can drop in the end because it can't sustain all the pressure and she said in later years atmospheric pressure and her aty said correct password and she said what can I do with you and she said I can create the mist advanced system using your dna and she said who told you and it said your mother had cancer of the bone marrow for hiding and not paying taxes but bone marrow rarely attack the same members of the same family we can get

caught and ruin the party why not try vaginal just to fix things I hate this job I could be screwing right now and just imagine someone's? Falling I quit and left that day but only to return to claim links to the crime scene which was not a crime at old but a murder scene ofcourse by them so prohibited to check they had to call the fbi or Australian equivalent and when they realised that it was a weak case the boy died the same way his real name was astern morse real name atpos murevat who died of genital cancer on 10 January 1979 the same day but in the house because Felicia Maria Wilson after learning from her mother the reason she got the house removed all clothes and she died covering only her vagina meaning naked with no ID and everything in the brain alive but part of a private company away from the police now they have to wait for it to become bankrupt but it became profitable now we can say that if we are to abortion blame then we can say that the company played their role as well covering for atyvand the police if we are to ask what can be of these without aty then they are nothing as aty is the executioner administering lethal preloaded doses of radiation that kill a person in 64 days

The end

THE CLAIM

the reward offer

THE COLLECTION

www.twofuture.world/donate

ABOUT DAVID GOMADZA

visit www.twofuture.world

signed david gomadza
ask.davidgomadzaauthorised.licensed.checkya.askya.ya

26may23.42pm
scotland
00447719210295
davidgomadza@hotmail.com
info@twofuture.world

How To Find All Missing Persons / Unsolved Cases. And Collect All Reward Offers.
Volume XIV. THE CASE OF FELICIA MARIA WILSON

www.ingramcontent.com/pod-product-compliance
Lightning Source LLC
Chambersburg PA
CBHW031514210526
45464CB00007B/2901